Darkroom Elegies

for Jackie

Darkroom Elegies
Concerning the Life and Work of Tina Modotti
Michael Shepler

Published 2009 by
Smokestack Books
PO Box 408, Middlesbrough TS5 6WA
e-mail : info@smokestack-books.co.uk
www.smokestack-books.co.uk

Darkroom Elegies
Michael Shepler
Copyright 2009 Michael Shepler, all rights reserved
Cover photo: *Falce pannocchia cartuccera* by Tina Modotti.
Every effort has been made to trace the copyright holders of
this photo. The author and publishers would be glad to hear
from copyright holders they have not been able to contact and
print due acknowledgement in the next edition.

Printed by
EPW Print & Design Ltd

ISBN 978-0-9554028-9-0
Smokestack Books gratefully
acknowledges the support of
Arts Council England

Smokestack Books is
represented by Inpress Ltd
www.inpressbooks.co.uk

Contents

- 9   Immigrant
- 10 Were You Aware of Me?
- 12 A Studio in Tropico, 1920
- 13 Movie
- 14 Tina & Robo
- 15 Snow in Hollywood, 1921
- 16 Robo de Richey, 1922
- 17 Picking Up the Camera, Mexico 1923
- 19 Tina Speaks of Mella
- 20 Los Angeles, 1926
- 22 The Assassination of Mella
- 23 Vittorio Vidali
- 24 Berlin, 1930
- 25 Weston, 1931
- 27 Europa, Russia
- 28 Moscow, 1931
- 30 Weston, 1936
- 32 Tina and Vittorio in Madrid, 1936
- 35 1937
- 36 The Tall Chimneys of Perpignan, 1939
- 38 The Camps
- 39 Stasova's Report, 1942
- 41 Tina, Mexico 1941
- 42 Vidali, Winter 1941
- 44 Charon's Taxi, 1942
- 46 Stasova Writes from Moscow, Winter 1942
- 47 Gallery, 1943
- 49 20th Congress of the CPSU, 1956
- 51 Vidali Growing Old
- 52 Rivera, 1946
- 54 After & Way After
- 55 Epilogue
- 56 Notes

Dramatis Personae

Tina Modotti (1896-1942)
Actress, model, photographer, revolutionary. Born Udine, Italy, died Mexico City. Agent of Red Aid during the Spanish Civil War 1936-1939.

Robo de Richey (1892-1922)
American painter and poet. Part of the Bohemian scene in California. Common-law-husband of Tina Modotti. Left California about the time she began her affair with Edward Weston. Died of smallpox in Mexico City.

Edward Weston (1886-1958)
American photographer. Lover and teacher of Tina Modotti. Followed her to Mexico City where she acted as his model, muse, manager and pupil before she took up photography herself in 1923. Left Mexico and Tina in 1926.

Diego Rivera (1886-1964)
Mexican painter and muralist. Husband of Frida Kahlo. Modotti modelled for two of Rivera's murals. Following his expulsion from the Mexican Communist Party he was associated with Trotsky's Fourth International.

Julio Mella (1905-1929)
Cuban revolutionary in exile. Romantically linked with Tina. She was at his side when he was assassinated, most probably by agents of Cuba's dictator, Geraldo Machado.

Vittorio Vidali (1900-1983)
Born Trieste. Agitator, writer, Comintern agent and soldier. Vidali and Modotti were a couple from 1930 until her death in 1942. Vidali was a Communist Senator in post-war Italy.

Elena Stasova (1873-1966)
Lifelong revolutionary. Personal secretary to Lenin. Later served with Red Aid. Probably saved the lives of Modotti and Vidali on two occasions by posting them to Europe during Stalin's purges in the 1930s and aiding their return to Mexico after the defeat of the Spanish Republic in 1939.

'Estos dias azules y este so de la infancia'

Immigrant

At 6:04 the black blossoms
Of umbrellas begin
Moving like a brigade
Of wintry sombreros.

At 6:05 I sit at the window;
The hole really; pounded out
Of an adobe wall with
An artist's chisel, with the
Glitter & weave of
A 1000 spider webs in place of
Glass.

Someone speaks to me in Spanish
Or Italian. I no longer know.

I no longer wonder where
The dream leads.
Narrow streets, shiny with rain.
The voice of an owl
High in the shuddering leaves.

My papers will never be
In order.

& although once again, I pass
To safety, I hear that Great Beast,
The century,
Roaring at my back.

Were you aware of me?

The shadow
Among shadows, who saw you,
Still a child, that hot afternoon
In Udine

& chose, from that brief glimpse,
To follow you all your days
& nights?

Silent, I watched
All your personas, your
Loves, fall away:

Yet I remained,
Leaning against the doors
Of a hundred sundown rooms.
Trailing ahead in the heat
Of noon; falling behind
In the quiet hour
Before nightfall.

My darkness
Cooling the wall
Of an outdoor café
In Vienna, Barcelona,
Trieste.

Drugged by your nearness
I grew forgetful
& you eluded me.

How I blackened the alleys
& streets of that
Seaside town in search
Of you!
If I'd lost you I would have
Left the world
In permanent Midnight.

Yet suddenly, there you were -
Bargaining with a street peddler.

Am I one of your ghosts?
Am I Mella?
Weston?
Am I Vittorio?

The man from the
Secret Police?

Can you kiss a shadow?
Can you whisper my name?

A Studio in Tropico, 1920

Gomez Robelo's book, *Satirios y Amores*, illustrated by
Robo de Richey, contains a pen & ink portrait of
Murder. The nude odalisque in Spanish lace
Has plunged her dagger deep into the heart
Of her lover.

Is this Tina? Is this the final warp of the original dream?
She hides her laughing face
Behind a black silk fan.

Movie

A banquet of shadow, light
& silence spreading out
Before our eyes as we drown
In your eyes

As you step
Out of
The moving mirror
Of tinted nitrate
We almost hear
Above the piano's somber drift
The jangle of your bracelets
As you open your arms

4 films, omitting the rumored *Greed*
By then you were with Weston
In Mexico

Heroine of *The Tiger's Coat* -
For the most part
They cast you as exotics

This dream slept, an unmarked reel
In the drowse of a downtown warehouse
On Olive, in LA

Until, one day
The owner torched it
For the insurance

Tina & Robo

The November 1921 issue of *California Southland*
Carried Seely's photo of you & Robo, heads lowered,
Quietly working in your small studio
On the Batiks you hoped to sell to the stars.

Preoccupied. Were you both thinking of Weston?
Or was it only Tina? Remembering
Last Sunday at his studio in Glendale
With the late sun pouring in.

The wine, spilled bright across her hands
Like a woman's blood when
The tide was ripe & the waves
Shuddered against the rough skin
Of the shore.

The way his beard
Felt like the wet, giving grit
Of beach line.

Nights when the moon was ripe.

Snow in Hollywood, 1921

It snowed in Hollywood in January 1921.
Snow. & the Aurora Borealis burning
Over Los Angeles in 1921.

Evenings at Zeitlins,
Robo & Tina, Twenties Beats
Orbiting Bohemian L.A.
Spilled rice wine & the music of Sarasate.

& you are with Weston now.
Weston's model,
Weston's lover,
Weston's muse.

He writes a friend:
'The pictures I believe to be especially good
Are of one Tina de Richey -
A lovely Italian girl.'

He shot you nude.
A geometry of curve & line.
Yet who could look
At those photos, & not,
For a moment,
Turn shyly away,
Like a boy at night,
Before an unguarded window,
Would look away, then back again.
& who could help but see,
in the dark of the mind,
Weston, in starched collar
& black suit -
His trim toothbrush moustache
Grazing the moist
Engulfing jungle
Atop your pubic bone.

Robo de Richey, 1922

Torn chapter from a discarded book.
Ragged, I flutter & clutch
The rough edge.

I recall coming awake
At the edge of Suicide Bridge.
It was late -
The dangerous hour when Souls
Float free -
Rising like the silk handkerchiefs of magicians.

Souls get lost at such an hour.
People die, or else just wake up.

Looking down into the Arroyo Seco
I see only blackness - a slow
Heavy Beast gathering.

I turn away,
Moving, not toward Eurydice,
Who'd become expendable,
But rather toward the scattered glow of Pasadena.

Past the startled eyes of cars,
Down Colorado, past Fair Oaks, Los Robles, Lake,
Closing inexorably on Sierra Madre
Where one last party faintly beckons.

Alone on the board, a tarnished knight,
I pass the Torch Club's eldritch light.

Picking Up the Camera, Mexico 1923

You tell Weston you're exhausted,
Staying home today.
You listen to the sharp slap of his huaraches as
He descends the stone steps.
For a while you're lulled, nailed flat;
Listening to the familiar sounds knocked loose
By the day's rising heat -

Wheels of a cart, a rooster crowing,
The bright voices of children.

Finally you have to move. You take Weston's
Spare camera, shopping for visions,
Strolling toward the wooden stalls of the Alameda.

& you will gather your visions swiftly, with quick ease.
A banquet of images -

Beginning in miniature,
The wooden vaquero with tall hat & lariat,
Hands of the Puppeteer - its tangle of wire & wood
& shadow strings;
The long hands & spidery fingers
Of the faceless puppeteer.

Or *Woman with Flag* (Palladian Print, 1928) - so vivid
Those who see it forever remember the flag as red.

The silver gelatin print of an unnamed girl - head bent,
Flower face intent, braided hair; braided beads encircling
Her small wrist.
All of 8, tracing
The twist & curl of new learned words
On the blank white page of her copy book.

2 kids guarding their parents stall
The boy in tilted cap, his poverty wrapped
In a lordly insolence.
Beside him - small heart face; everything
Drawing you into the brown depths
Of her eyes.

You can tell she'd die for him
& that he'd kill for her.

A six year bouquet,
Ending with the sharp punctuation of gunfire.

Finally the picture of Vidali on the deck of the Edam,
Heading home. Staring at the gathering maelstrom
With a benign smile.

& the last photo: Hansel & Gretel at the zoo -
Old now, large as hippos,
They've come to the monkey house to stare
At Nothing in its cage.

Neruda claimed one blustery morning in Moscow
He watched you toss your camera into the icy river.
An act, tragic as the lonely death
Of Rosa Luxemburg.

The great legends & the great lies
Eventually unmask, &, embracing like old actors,
Exit laughing.

Why did we think we needed them
When we have the rough facts of these photographs
Spread out before us?

Tina Speaks of Mella

The streets were still drowsy with siesta
& people were just beginning to move
Slowly, sluggishly, like bees
Through a hive, half-drunk with sleep
& heat.

If we'd had time we could have gone
To the open windows of the office
Of *El Machete*
Drinking in the sweet tasting air
Looking down on the bright
Corrupt world,

But we had a paper to get out
So we stayed at our typewriters
Heads down, fingers jabbing the keys -

A ceaseless song, spreading out
Through the room, each of us
A virtuoso, as Revolution's symphony
Circled the room, Intro to Coda,
Displacing the heavy air, flying
With red flame wings, through
The open windows
Soaring over shrine & pyramid,

& the door opened & you walked in
Out of the sun as if I'd conjured you.

Los Angeles, 1926

'Reality makes him dream'
(introduction to a book of Weston photographs)

Having returned from Mexico, Weston goes
To see Murnau's *The Last Laugh* at the Orpheum
Losing his mind in the night streets of Weimar

On screen, Jannings, deemed too old, too weak
To perform his duties as Doorman
At the Grand Hotel, turns his back
To the camera. Such thick sadness!
What treacherous harpoon could lay this
Great Beast low?

Is Weston drawn to the fluidity of Murnau's dream?
A thousand stills made animate float through
The cavernous brain of the Dreamers in the dark.
Hypnogogic light - like the glint
Of Mesmer's twirling watch, plays across a thousand
Shuttering eyes

As each evening the old man sheds his lavatory attendant's smock
Retrieving his doorman's jacket, with its gold epaulettes
His stature increasing with each piece of cloth, until, resplendent
As the Kaiser, he leaves the hotel, crossing the city
To his own dank street
& he swaggers now, past the awestruck neighbors

He swaggers, but with a limp

A crippled spider, legs moving sidewise
In the effort to reach the apex
Of its thick-spun web
'Do they see it?' the Doorman thinks
& Weston hears him thinking

& Weston, too, is drifting
Becoming insubstantial as dust
Whirling in the dry light of a Magic Lantern
Thoughts fragmenting, half dreaming

He sees Tina standing by an open door
Tina - acting again, the Doorman's daughter
Pregnant, & then a suicide
Cold & small -
Alone on a steel table in a room
In the centre of the Labyrinth where he'd left her.

The Assassination of Mella

The heavy grey sky of exile
Crushes me.
The way the weight of the sea
Crushes a diver gone down too far.

All I remember, all that is worth
Recollection, I left on that beleaguered island,
My Cuba.

Tonight, Tina is on my arm
& we're leaving the office of El Machete
To meet Magriñat, or Death himself, who owns
These ill-lit streets.
& though he's only 14, an itinerant actor
On a cattle boat bound for Ireland, years away
From even holding a camera, the eye
Is that of Welles - the unholy tilt of these midnight streets
Bear his mark.

We can see the light pouring out of the cantina.
Songs of murder fill the street like
Glittering mist. The tinny piano, each of its
Keys propels the skeletal dance
As the last grains pass through the glass
& the moon is veiled by clouds.

A burning pain seems to precede the shots.
I hear them, faintly, like far off fireworks.
Two quick bursts as I'm falling - feeling
Nothing but two sharp stabs, & Tina's
Hand, & my hand slipping through it
& her screaming.

Just faces now. A circle of curious faces.
I try to speak - 'Machado killed me.'

The three words seem to separate from each
Other - growing meaningless
In their isolation.

Vittorio Vidali

1927. Paralyzed by the tumult of Babylon America, its weeks before he can write again.
The sorrow, the memory of leaving Moscow, reminded him that his life consisted of
Trains, stations, steamers, arrivals, departures.

This evening he writes to his friend Nino in Italy. He writes from the shanty-slums
Of Riga - an agent of the Comintern, hidden among immigrants, his great wish,
To move straight to the goal, to walk, to fight, love. To deserve the love of his
Comrades, &, if he must, to fall side by side with the others.

From Riga he travels to Mexico, back to the Soviet Union, then Spain & Mexico
Again. He is a survivor. A Red patriarch who goes home finally to Italy where
He writes his memoirs, laughs, loves, sleeps the peaceful sleep of the violent
Man who is able to justify his violence.

He wakes late among the olive trees & walks slowly home, guided by the red
Light of Mars.

Berlin, 1930

Forest of iron & lights.

The sputtering bulbs of electric stars
Flare & dim, casting a livid glow
On faces Kollwitz might have painted.

At windwracked stands headlines snarl
In Deutsch. Each word,
Rough. Black. Bestial.

& no eyes lift toward the velvet sky
Of tinselled heaven. & none hear
The creak of the cheap wings of
The poor lifting aloft;
Fresh from a pawnshop,
The pattern robbed from Icarus.
How many even cleared the rotted fence
Of their death?

All eyes remain fixed on the hard asphalt street,
Tracing the fast moving feet, the wheels of
Cabs, the horse hooves of mounted police,

The chipped gutter with its iron drain & vertical bars
& the papers blowing by like fluttering ghosts, flyers
Advertising bicycle races, boxing matches,
Street fights.

The city is a range of spectral towers.
Its lights come on, dressing it out
Like an ancient whore on Saturday night.

Everywhere, cold hate, black boots.
The feel of time running out.

Weston, 1931

No letters since you left Berlin.
The room is suffocating. I throw on
My coat & rush outside.

I turn the corner &, pausing, realize
That, against all reason, I am listening
For your footsteps.

The bright step which cleared away Darkness

I had been sitting on the 'hypo' barrel
In the dim green light of my darkroom,
Reflecting on the past, & pondering
The future.

It always comes back to you.

All I can see are your eyes.
I drown in your eyes.

All I can see are your lips,
I bite your lips, tasting the thick

Blood of the earth.

Your hair is black;
Heavy as the sleep which only comes
after a day of hard labor.

I bury my thoughts in the oblivion
Of your black hair.

Solitary walker, drifting through
The quiet city -
Past manicured lawns

& the hiss of sprinklers turning
All night in an effort to hold back
The desert.

I glance toward the jagged line
Of the San Gabriels.
Fog threads the ravines
Tangling in the tall trees.

Europa, Russia

Faded stickers emboss
The sides of battered
Luggage & its fake leather
Skin - rough & peeling.
This is the train of dreams
Or nightmares. The slow train
Of history, which halts,
Breaks down, snorting fire
Through iron nostrils, its head
Forward, a maddened bull,
Its black sides slick with oil
& blood, its one yellow
Eye beamed straight ahead,
The Orient Express drives
Deeper into sleet, rain.
The icebreaker rips
Through centuries, opens
Haemophilic veins
With the applied pressure
Of its surgical snout.
We're rushing past bonfires
Where only darkness reigned before.
The Czar. Little Father.
Absent parent. Landlord
Of everything.
Goodbye. Goodbye. Goodbye.

Moscow, 1931

The lights on in daylight
& the banners flying.

Later, Neruda would tell the story
Of how you'd asked the driver
To stop a moment. Of how,
Unhesitatingly, you'd thrown
The Graflex into the Moscow River,
Got back in the cab & proceeded
To the Hotel Lux with your credentials:
Comrade Modotti: Representative of Red Aid.

You've gone so long without sleep
That waking has lost its meaning.
Everything had become dreams,
Parables, stories, true & untrue,
Grey as an unravelled bandage
When the blood's soaked through.

& so quiet you can hear
The guard's footsteps
In the Kremlin courtyard.

You see the Evening Star, a red tip
On the end of his bayonet.
You see, in a row of high windows,
An isolate light -
Is it really he?

In rumpled tunic, sleepless as you
Bent at his desk, 150 pounds
Of damaged steel - lamplight framing
His pockmarked face -
Jack-o-Lantern man, former seminarian
The scratch of his pen
As he churns out treatise, poem, death warrant.
Eager to drive the world deeper
Into the cleansing flames.

& then you remember
The man in the dark blue suit
Wearing dark blue eyeshades,
In the yellow window of the passing train.
Rushing through dark blue
He'd looks as if he was dreaming.
Dreaming & racing toward his death.
A firing squad in dark blue.
Even their shadows
Even the shiny barrels
Dark blue.

The rumpled man picks up his phone -
'Vidali? Is it you?'

'Hello, Triggerman', he says.

Weston, 1936

An army of ants marches in a straight line
Across the rough boards of my kitchen table.
Marches purposefully toward some intuited destination
Kept secret from me.

Thoughts of Tina. Tina on the first day & the last.
The final letter, written in her hand, yes,
But in a code as impenetrable to me
As the language of the ants.

I had to leave Mexico because, even in
Its liveliness, the subtext was always death.
Yet I curse myself - pathetic priest, worshipping
The fixed images of constructed art. Hedonist &
Isolato; forever split.

I recall how at parties, Tina & I often went
Disguised as one another, & how later, in love,
Undressing her was undressing myself.
She'd lift the bright dress over my head
& for a moment all was darkness
As she bit my nipples, & I jammed
The coloured cloth in my mouth
To keep from screaming.

I had to leave Mexico.

& in leaving, returned to what now seemed
The Old World, with riches that would have shamed
The Conquistadors.

If only it weren't for the Blackness.
Not the black magic of the darkroom,
But a black Nada, heavy & cold at the core of me.
A longing for something lost.

When I think of her. When I think of us,
I remember Machado's poem:

'Y cuando llegue el dia del ultimo viaje,
y este al partir la nave que nunca ha de tornar,
me encontrareis a bordo ligero de equipaje,
casi desnudo, como los hijos de la mar.'

Tina & Vittorio in Madrid, 1936

Staring at an ill-lit contrail
Arrowing above the morning
Star

I recollect 1936: the year
Karloff made a second, fatal attempt
To harness the power of Andromeda -
(for 'Good' of course).

As Carlos (his *nom de guerre*)
& Maria (that's Herself)
Viewed the makeshift barricades
At the edges of Madrid.

They travelled a different route to Spain -
Skirting the Carpathian observatory
Where Boris ministered to his blind mother,
Neglecting his lovely wife, 'Frances Drake'
(her *nom de cinema*) - stunning in velvet cloak,
Who hurries to meet the scoffing scientists
& lead them to the laboratory.

Carlos & Maria are talking quietly
To a small group of men &
Milicianas; inspecting a machine-gun
Left over from the war against the Riffs.

'Colonialism has come to our aid', Carlos quips.

Points of No Return are being reached
& its as if everyone were asleep -

The scientists, the combatants, the few
Sheepish star-gazers, their cell phones gone dead,

Adrift in the 21st Century, bereft of once-promised
Utopias -

Buck Rogers a poorly drawn cartoon after all
Zarkoff & Ming plying Dale Arden
With sinister drinks - see! Her tunic's unbuttoned!

Soon we'll hear the plangent horns
Of Franco's goons, the Moors.
They'll come screaming down the street,
Falling by the dozens before our guns -

& the next wave & the next.

As Carlos quickly, ruthlessly, forges the workers
Into the 5th Regiment, through violence,
Discipline, & force of personality.

On the nights of November 6-7 he interrogates
A thousand suspected 5th columnists -
Most are executed.
When he emerges from the prison
On the morning of the 8th, his thumb
& trigger finger are charred black
From powder burns.

Day after day Madrid holds.

***

Meanwhile, Karloff's experiment backfires again
('Some things we're not meant to know!')
& he's transformed into a human lightbulb
Whose touch is death.

Frances Drake, distraught, falls for a feckless
Explorer who 'single handedly mapped the
Mountains of the Moon'.

He's mapping her mountains with both hands
When, in a snit, Neon Boris incinerates everybody.
The audience shuffles outside,
Vanishing into the long night of the Depression.

Bums line park benches with headlines
About Madrid.

Here, in 2006, we feather our nests
As best we can; peek 'neath the bed
In search of Moors & Riffs,
&, having scared ourselves silly,
Relinquish our hopes.

Our dreams go hungry -

No Dale Arden, No Frances Drake
To lay us to waste.

Just the bums in the park.
The Stygian bonfires of Madrid.

1937

The low droning moan of death going away.
Soft as a breeze, the dark wings tilt
& the sun is gone, eclipsed by rising particles
Of dust, a thousand tons, each speck
Light as a child's whisper, rising & rising.

Mussolini's nephew described dropping bombs
On Ethiopia 'like a red rose opening'.

We can see it too, from the equable floating distance;
The numb high equability of shock's first plateau.

The schoolmaster, his head twisted to one side,
Resting on the bosom of Rosa the fishmonger.
The novice nun, her black habit high above
Her pale parted thighs.

Worst though, are the children & the animals:
The horse & bull; the agony no picador
Could tease with his lance.
The blinkered pain as the horn hooks through
The pleated cloth worn to spare the spectator's
Sensibilities.
That ignoble moment, worse than death, in the sand
On Sunday afternoon.

The village transfigured into a smouldering ring
Of slow suffering death. A shell-shocked bird
Begins singing. His song is strange,
Like the siren shriek that came too late.
Other singers join in; a choir of amateurs,
Ashamed to give voice to such elevated feelings.
No one asked for or even guessed
Their calamitous fate. Even the suicidal barber,
His mind darkened by images of his wife's adultery -
Thoughts of a bloody razor spilling liquid fire,
Couldn't have dreamt or wished these last few hours.

The Tall Chimneys of Perpignan, 1939

At first, cold silence. Then the brittle, wintry
Cries of crows & the grumble
Of the Garde Mobile behind you.

Low company exchanging low tales,
Trading lies; complaining
To God or anyone who'd listen;
Cursing the cold in that beautiful language
Which could turn the worst curse into a
Blessing.

You cup your hands around the flaring match -
The brittle coal of the cigarette-end glitters,
Widening like the red eye
Of Polyphemus, startled suddenly awake.

The first faint figures appear on the
Frozen rim, motionless
An instant before beginning the slow
Descent into neutral territory & the
Benign prison that is France.

Now more figures spill over the top,
Blending into a shadow column
That comes on all day & past sundown,
Ragged as the smoke curling from
The tall chimneys of Perpignan.

Days before Barcelona fell, you begged Carlos to rescue the poet,
Machado, one of the strongest voices of Spain.

Carlos is among the last to cross.
You see him, coming down the last steep grade;
Slow, reluctant. You expect him to turn back,
Yet finally he comes on,
Tossing aside rifle & side arm, yet clutching the
Knotted red bandana with its sweet burden of
Spanish earth.

He tells you Machado is dead in Collioure,
Reciting his last lines, found in the pocket
Of the old man's coat:

'Estos dias azules y este sol de la infancia'

'Move along', the guard says.
You are already vanishing
Into the blue evening.

The Camps

Argeles-sur-mer, St.-Cyrian, La Lozere, Las Haras, Aude, Agde, St.-Etienne, Le Vernet, Gurs, Sept Fonts, Arles-sur-tech, Chateau due Colliore, La Reynarde, Chateau de Mont-grande, Le Perthus, Herault, Haute-Garonne, Mazeres, Le Boulou, Prats de Molio, St.-Laurent-de Cerdans, Le Tour de Carol, Bourg-Madame, Mount Louis

The largest of the French internment camps were on the beach 400,000 behind the wire

No food No barracks No blankets No beds

Only wind & sand

Liberte. Egalite. Fraternite.

Stasova's Report, 1942

Tina & Vidali.
Impulsive. Both of them.
Always eager for the
Great Risk.
'The Greater the risk
For the greatest good'.
You could hear it,
See it, a shining phrase
Behind the eyes.
She turned down the
Position of official
Photographer for
The Party.
Perhaps realizing
How easily what might
Be developed
Could also be erased.
Cropped. Shot.
Or lost amongst
The mute decay of
Dusty boxes,
Banished to wait
Forever. Denied
The swift luxury of
The furnace's
Obliteration.

She had no wish to become
One of those nameless
Doctors who lobotomized
History.

Somehow, they came to
Sorge's attention.
Probably through Vidali.

A swashbuckler & an
Artist! An old combo
But they steadied one
Another. Perhaps that's
What Sorge thought
When he seeded their
Dreams with the liberation
Of Manchuko.

I saved them - sending
Them to Spain.
How could I have known
The Boss's fear of
Contagion would flourish to include
Exposure to lost causes?
Somehow I managed to post
Them to Mexico.

I think then, Tina
Was already dying
From the wounds
Of Spain.
But Vittorio never changed.
Spain was only one battle
In the war.
Trotsky, he knew, was
In Mexico - a flame
To be smothered.
Yet a flame which cast
A long shadow.

Tina, Mexico 1941

It's been such a time getting here;
Trucks & trains,
Houses, safe & unsafe;
A long run across guarded borders,
Eyes keen for an opening,
A tear in the fence,
&, in an instant, we are passing the last guards,
Faint as the slight breeze which stirs
Our invisible cloaks; & then years pass.

We have the sunlight, the vast space;
We have our work, which tires us out;
The rich tiredness a farmer feels,
Walking back from his sown field,
Coming back to the single light
Of his house; or, on Saturday evening,
To the bright talk of the exile's café.

Someday we'll return.
Things won't be as we'd remembered them
In the days before the dark,
But they'll be good just the same.
For now though, we're among friends,
Laughing at how we got over.

Vidali, Winter 1941

I was picked up in the last narrow street
Before reaching home.

Four men. Mexican police,
Looking little different from officers
Of the SIM.

Their eyes wordlessly communicating
A single concrete thought:

They will do whatever is necessary
To get the information they want.

They will repeat the procedures
Again & again
Until you're dead
Or broken.

'Are you taking me for a ride?'
I asked the one next to me
In the backseat of the dusty Packard.

I imagine you know his answer.

Forty days & forty nights,
Biblical as the Flood,.
They held me in the foetid shithole
Of El Pocito.

Only 3 weeks you say?

Time enough to recite from memory
The complete works of Neruda.

To remember the bodies, not the names,
Of every woman I'd ever had;
Or loved & had;
Or loved & never had.

As I'd suspected, their boots & fists
Were no harder or more persuasive than Il Duce's,

& I'd exhausted them & given them nothing,
& suddenly I was free.

Charon's Taxi, 1942

You're late leaving the small gathering of exiles
(Who would call it a party, though there was
Wine, laughter & talk, too many silenced
Voices were speaking in the twist
& rise of smoke greying the room)

Past midnight, & a light rain whispers blessings
On the shiny cobbled empty streets.

You're holding what might be an artist's portfolio
Tight against your body, & it's too dark to see
How beautiful you are - or were.
Beneath the lamplight we only see
The shadow-sculpted lines,
The gouged arroyos of tears.

You'd walked away from Vittorio; leaving him deep
In conversation & song - imagining you could smell
Blood on his heavy carpenter's hands.

Now, hailing a late cab, you only want to be home,
Away from the poverty, the memories
Of this street, where Mella was shot down -
The gun so close
The powder burns spread across
His forehead like a charred birthmark,

& your hands were covered with blood,
Hands like startled doves,
Fluttering, as you tried to brush the blood
From your skirts.

You remember the long march
Through Mexico City's streets -
A forest of red banners like leaves blazing
In late autumn.

The silent cabbie has the radio loud -
'La Paloma', rancheras.

You slump, stunned, as if punched
In the chest, as a cloud moulds the moon
Into an Aztec knife.

History buries her actors deep.

Once a year someone remembers.
Their tears watering the old roses
In the tilted vase on your grave.

Stasova Writes From Moscow, Winter 1942

Week after week the siege of Stalingrad goes on.
The city is rubble yet the battle continues
& the tide begins to turn.
Soon 'Field Marshal Winter' shall play
His infallible stratagem
& the spine of Paulus's army will snap.

I have a wish, a hope.

That out of this cold abattoir
The Red Phoenix will emerge reborn.
The Idea - revitalized by war's glowing forge.

Oh Tina! If you were here,
I you could witness it!

Gallery, 1943

Clumsy dancers, they hobble long halls
On broken legs. Eyes lifting briefly
Like broken wings.

Voices praising faintly.
Small mouths whispering.

*Sound of soft rain on damp leaves
in an untended garden
at the far borders
of a quiet town*

'I quite like this one!'
'I quite like that one!'

*the sea of sombreros shot from a rooftop,
May 1925*

*scarred hands grasping a shovel
machete, sickle & cartridge belt*

*the pelado crashed on the pavement
beneath the smooth gent in the tux
on the paint-peeled billboard*

*Mella's typewriter in the El Machete office
afternoon sun threading through a dirty window
striking the keys, the faded ribbon, the
half-finished polemic, with its few, discernable words:
'Inspiracion. Artistica. Sintesis.'*

Yet their lack of enthusiasm is deceptive.
The rich are notorious for their lack of enthusiasm,
Yet the rich can pay.

By the time the old janitor, with mop & bucket,
Has completed his nightly ballet, each photo
Will be labeled 'Sold'.

Carefully locking up, he lets himself out.
Owning nothing himself, he knows the value
Placed on Property.

It's the hour when night turns toward morning.
Fog softens the streets, muffling his footsteps
As he crosses the plaza.

20th Congress of the CPSU, 1956

'How many railway stations I've seen in my lifetime!'
(Vittorio Vidali)

Malenkov spoke a great deal about electrification
& quoted Lenin;
He spoke of the Nuclear Age
& energy problems;
But I
Just
Didn't
Feel
Like
Listening
To
Him.

Each morning, leaving my room for the day's round of sessions
& speeches, I thought of my fellow countryman's long voyage
Through the nether regions & wondered
Where my Virgil was? Dead? Exiled?

The Omitted One still lingered in the great hall.
You could smell his sweat, the pungent scent
Of his tobacco; &, between speech & silence,
You even thought you heard
The low cough of his laughter -
Cold as a breeze twisting up from
An unfilled grave.

Yet each day was drenched by the slow boiling waves
Of Change.

& the unceasing waves of applause were drowning
That laughter.
Words of men

Like Togliatti, Duclos, Thorez;
Ghost words of Luxemburg, Gramsci, Lenin -
Rich as dark earth, a steady pattering rain of words
Hitting a steel casket,
Drowning the Great Fear.

Vidali Growing Old

Remember the Schutstaffel Colonel in *Open City?*
His neat desk. Black thinning hair skinned back:
A Death's head.

Remember the black pins that covered
The streets & districts on the wall map of Rome?
Each a point of Resistance.

Remember the pleasure he took, removing them,
One by one, just as he did when he was
Removing fingernails, breaking hands…

My enemy. Yet I understood him.

I prowled Madrid all night with a long barrelled pistol.
The smell of cordite in my clothes.
The barrel was painted red,
I have it here somewhere.

I remember when Olmo picked it up by mistake,
Carrying it into the kitchen. The boy was eight.
How his mother shrieked!

I laughed, tossing him over my shoulder.
'This is no toy', I told him.
'Not for little boys.'

Rivera, 1946

They couldn't get my murals out of their minds
Not the spectators, not my enemies, not the women
Not the Central Committee

'Unreliable. Undisciplined.' These were some of the more
Polite phrases bandied about when Wolfe managed
To have me thrown out of the Party
'Distracting' was another - & perhaps more to the point

High on my scaffold, oblivious to intrigue, I painted joyously
How could I help firing my pistol in the air on occasion?
Fame & Revolution, I believed, could go hand in hand

Tina was there every day - recording my progress
With her Graflex, posing for *The Abundant Earth*
Weston knew sparks were flying, but he was enmeshed
In his own dream of Mexican splendour -
Shooting everything - 3 days fascinated, he photographed
All angles & aspects of a porcelain commode
Haunting the streets, the pulquerias, befriending Firmin
Before the Fall, when he was still British Consul to Mexico

One evening at El Farolito, Firmin insisted Weston come home with him
To photograph Yvonne
(Yvonne, who'd travelled south to recuperate from Hollywood)

While Firmin hallucinated the great misshapen head
Of Popo, ghostly through the gauze, looming
Above his cuckold's bed like the head of my dead twin
Or the endless rows of sugar skulls jammed in bins
At the marketplace -
Cheap sweet Memento Mori of life's grinning holocaust

After Weston was gone; poisoned by the space
& thin air; Tina posed for me again - a soldadera
In *The Arsenal*, passing out ammunition
A leather belt of bullets feeding from her hands
Through Mella's hands while Vidali, in black suit
& black Trilby, hovered behind them

It was as if I'd foretold their Fate
Or so it must have seemed to those who believe such things
You can believe I stayed close by her during that bad time
Following the death of Mella
Of course, later we fell out
But then I fell out with everyone
I was a buffoon! A fantasist! A traitor!

None saw that I was merely a dreamer
Sleepwalking through the wistful lives of phantoms
& all of them, even Frida,
Were colours in my paintbox -
To be used or squandered in the lifelong creation
Of the only reality to which I held allegiance

After & Way After

The Mythmaker has summoned me back
Hoping another glance might unmist
The mirror, capturing the truth of me,
Or at least,
The truth reflected.

I'm surprised as you.
Recall, I died in a cab's backseat
On a wintry Mexican street,
So near morning I cried, begging
One final dawn, one more fire.
So that now, having risen like a female Christ
I find myself embarrassed,
Unprepared.
An actress, robbed of her lines,
Can only reach into the dark.

Not every century has its Children's Crusade.
Perhaps I required a triumph.
Perhaps I was starving for victory.
Remembering the dogged patience
Of the old, crossing the mountains,
Fleeing Death, only to be met by Death
Speaking French.

Even in this dark room, the lamp
Still sways
& the vast diorama of years whirls past.

Something resembling my life
Sits in the cornered shadows, singing.

Epilogue

I have been waiting long enough to drink
3 cognacs. Long enough
To smoke six cigarettes.

The quiet sun hushes the passing wheels
Of a horse cart on the Calle Obregon.
The last few bees lift, heavy with honey.

Lengthening shadows lend a sinister sweetness
& when the evening lights come on
The crowds will step a bit faster,
As if chasing after the crisp autumnal leaves
That hurry & pile up
At the cemetery gate.

I don't need to consult my watch to know you aren't coming,
& I know that in a moment, I'll return to the hotel
& burn this message in the chipped porcelain basin.

I have a steamship ticket in my jacket pocket
& though its destination has disappeared
I am still able to take comfort in it.

'And when the day arrives for the final voyage
and the ship of no return is set to sail,
you'll find me aboard, traveling light,
almost naked, like the children of the sea.'

Antonio Machado

NOTES

A Studio in Tropico, 1920
The town of Glendale, California was previously named Tropico.

Movie
Modotti appeared in four silent films in 1921 and 1922, starring in *The Tiger's Coat*.

Snow in Hollywood, 1921
Jake Zeitlin owned a rare bookstore in Los Angeles, which was a gathering place for local writers and artists.

Robo de Richey, 1922
Robo de Richey died of small pox in Mexico in 1922. More than 100 people jumped to their deaths from the Colorado Street Bridge, which became known as 'Suicide Bridge'.

Tina Speaks of Mella
El Machete was the official paper of the Mexican Communist Party. Julio Mella was a Cuban communist, murdered by the dictator, Geraldo Machado.

The Assassination of Mella
Magrinat was a stool pigeon, probably in the pay of Machado.

Berlin 1930
Kathe Kollwitz (1867-1945) German artist.

Moscow 1931
Red Aid was an international social service organization connected to the Comintern. It was founded in 1922 to function as an 'international political Red Cross'. Red Aid conducted campaigns in support of communist prisoners and raised material and humanitarian support.

Weston, 1936
'And when the day arrives for the final voyage
and the ship of no return is set to sail,
you'll find me aboard, travelling light,
almost naked, like the children of the sea.'
(Antonio Machado)

Tina and Vittorio in Madrid, 1936
In the battle for Madrid the city was held by the 5th Regiment, commanded by Vittorio Vidali under his *nom de guerre* 'Commandant Carlos Contreras'. The movie referred to in the poem is *The Invisible Ray* with Boris Karloff and Frances Drake. Buck Rogers was a popular figure in comics and film.

The Tall Chimneys of Perpignan
'These blue days and this sun of childhood' (Antonio Machado).

The Camps
The names in the first stanza are those of the concentration camps in which Spanish refugees, fleeing Franco Spain, were held by the French authorities.

Stasova's Report, 1942
Victor Sorge was a Soviet agent who operated a highly successful spy ring in Japan from 1933 until his arrest in 1941

Vidali, Winter 1941
Vidali compares his treatment by the Mexican police with that of the SIM (Servicio de Inteligencia Militar), military intelligence service of the Republican government in Spain during the civil war.

20th Congress of the CPSU, 1956
Khruschev's 'secret speech' outlined the crimes of Stalin. The 20th Congress heralded a definitive break with Stalinism.

Rivera, 1946
Bertram Wolfe was a US communist living in Mexico, later a follower of Trotsky. *Abundant Earth* and *The Arsenal* were murals in which Modotti appeared. Geoffrey Firmin is the (fictional) protagonist of Malcolm Lowry's novel, *Under the Volcano*.

Vidali Growing Old
Roberto Rossellini's *Rome: Open City* (1945) is often described as the first neo-realist film.